W9-ANU-258

DATE DUE		

WEEKLY **WR** READER®

EARLY LEARNING LIBRARY

How Plants Grow/Cómo crecen las plantas

How Grass Grows/
Cómo crece la hierba

by/por Joanne Mattern

Reading consultant/Consultora de lectura:
Susan Nations, M.Ed.,
author, literacy coach,
and consultant in literacy development/
autora, tutora de alfabetización,
y consultora de desarrollo de la lectura

Please visit our web site at: www.earlyliteracy.cc
For a free color catalog describing Weekly Reader® Early Learning Library's list
of high-quality books, call 1-877-445-5824 (USA) or 1-800-387-3178 (Canada).
Weekly Reader® Early Learning Library's fax: (414) 336-0164.

Library of Congress Cataloging-in-Publication Data

Mattern, Joanne, 1963-
　[How grass grows. Spanish & English]
　How grass grows = cómo crecen la hierba / Joanne Mattern.
　　p. cm. — (How plants grow = cómo crecen las plantas)
　Includes bibliographical references and index.
　ISBN 0-8368-6462-X (lib. bdg.)
　ISBN 0-8368-6469-7 (softcover)
　1. Grasses—Growth—Juvenile literature.　2. Grasses—Development—
Juvenile literature.　I. Title.
QK495.G74M36618　2006
584'.9—dc22　　　　　　　　　　　　　　　　　2005032237

This edition first published in 2006 by
Weekly Reader® Early Learning Library
A Member of the WRC Media Family of Companies
330 West Olive Street, Suite 100
Milwaukee, WI　53212　USA

Managing editor: Valerie J. Weber
Art direction: Tammy West
Cover design and page layout: Kami Strunsee
Translators: Tatiana Acosta and Guillermo Gutiérrez
Picture research: Cisley Celmer

Picture credits: Cover, © Raymond Gehman/National Geographic Society Image Collection;
p. 5 © Yva Momatiuk and John Eastcott/Photo Researchers, Inc.; pp. 7, 9, 17 © Nigel Cattlin/
Holt Studios/Photo Researchers, Inc.; p. 11 © Stephen McBrady/PhotoEdit; p. 13 © Seizo Terasaki/
Stone/Getty Images; p. 15 Kami Strunsee/© Weekly Reader® Early Learning Library; p. 19 © Spencer
Grant/Photo Researchers, Inc.; p. 21 © age fotostock/SuperStock

Printed in the United States of America

1 2 3 4 5 6 7 8 9 10 09 08 07 06

Note to Educators and Parents

Reading is such an exciting adventure for young children! They are beginning to integrate their oral language skills with written language. To encourage children along the path to early literacy, books must be colorful, engaging, and interesting; they should invite the young reader to explore both the print and the pictures.

How Plants Grow is a new series designed to introduce young readers to the life cycle of familiar plants. In simple, easy-to-read language, each book explains how a specific plant begins, grows, and changes.

Each book is specially designed to support the young reader in the reading process. The familiar topics are appealing to young children and invite them to read — and reread — again and again. The full-color photographs and enhanced text further support the student during the reading process.

In addition to serving as wonderful picture books in schools, libraries, homes, and other places where children learn to love reading, these books are specifically intended to be read within an instructional guided reading group. This small group setting allows beginning readers to work with a fluent adult model as they make meaning from the text. After children develop fluency with the text and content, the book can be read independently. Children and adults alike will find these books supportive, engaging, and fun!

— Susan Nations, M.Ed., author, literacy coach,
and consultant in literacy development

Nota para los maestros y los padres

¡Leer es una aventura tan emocionante para los niños pequeños! A esta edad están comenzando a integrar su manejo del lenguaje oral con el lenguaje escrito. Para animar a los niños en el camino de la lectura incipiente, los libros deben ser coloridos, estimulantes e interesantes; deben invitar a los jóvenes lectores a explorar la letra impresa y las ilustraciones.

Cómo crecen las plantas es una nueva colección diseñada para presentar a los jóvenes lectores el ciclo de vida de plantas muy conocidas. Cada libro explica, en un lenguaje sencillo y fácil de leer, cómo nace, se desarrolla y cambia una planta específica.

Cada libro está especialmente diseñado para ayudar a los jóvenes lectores en el proceso de lectura. Los temas familiares llaman la atención de los niños y los invitan a leer — y releer — una y otra vez. Las fotografías a todo color y el tamaño de la letra ayudan aún más al estudiante en el proceso de lectura.

Además de servir como maravillosos libros ilustrados en escuelas, bibliotecas, hogares y otros lugares donde los niños aprenden a amar la lectura, estos libros han sido especialmente concebidos para ser leídos en un grupo de lectura guiada. Este contexto permite que los lectores incipientes trabajen con un adulto que domina la lectura mientras van determinando el significado del texto. Una vez que los niños dominan el texto y el contenido, el libro puede ser leído de manera independiente. ¡Estos libros les resultarán útiles, estimulantes y divertidos a niños y a adultos por igual!

— Susan Nations, M.Ed., autora, tutora de alfabetización, y
consultora de desarrollo de la lectura

There are many kinds of grass. Some grasses grow on prairies. Some grow in your yard.

Hay muchos tipos de hierba. Algunos crecen en las praderas. Otros crecen en tu jardín.

5

Grass grows from seeds.

La hierba nace de
las semillas.

Dirt covers the seed. Roots grow from the seed down into the dirt.

- - - - - - - - - - - - - - - - - -

La tierra cubre la semilla. De la semilla nacen raíces que penetran en la tierra.

root/raíz

Roots get water and food from the dirt.

Las raíces toman agua y alimento de la tierra.

A **stem** grows from the seed.
Soon it pushes up through
the dirt.

De la semilla brota un **tallo**.
Pronto, el tallo se abre paso
y sale de la tierra.

stem/tallo

Some grasses have **crowns**.
Special kinds of stems grow
down from the crown.

Algunas hierbas tienen
una **corona**. De la corona
salen unos tipos especiales
de tallos.

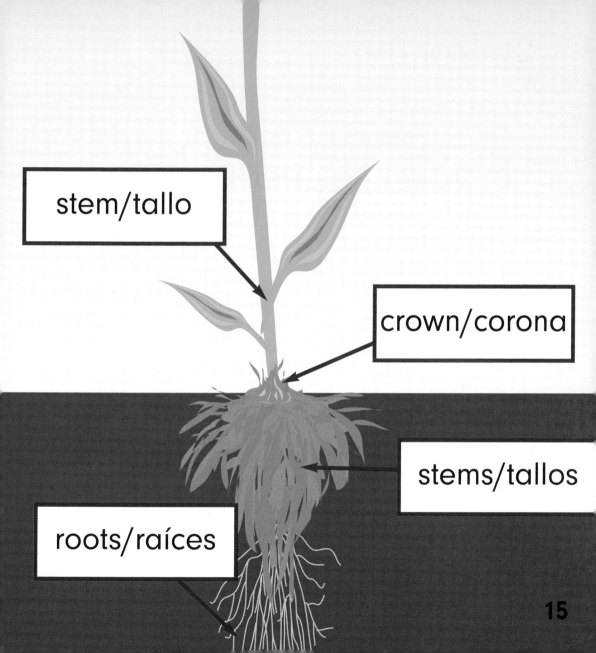

stem/tallo

crown/corona

stems/tallos

roots/raíces

15

The crown lies near the top of the dirt.

La corona está cerca de la superficie de la tierra.

17

Mowing the grass cuts the stems. It does not cut the crown. So new grass always grows!

Cuando pasamos la podadora, cortamos los tallos. No cortamos la corona. ¡Por eso, la hierba vuelve a crecer!

Does the grass feel good on your toes?

¿Te gusta pisar la hierba?

Glossary

crown — the part of grass where the stems grow
prairies — lands filled with wild grasses
roots — parts of a plant that grow under the ground
seeds — parts of a plant that grow into new plants
stem — the part of a plant where leaves and
flowers grow

Glosario

corona — parte de la hierba de donde salen
los tallos
praderas — tierras cubiertas de hierbas silvestres
raíces — partes de la planta que crecen bajo
la tierra
semillas — partes de una planta que se
convierten en nuevas plantas
tallo — parte de la planta de donde salen las
hojas y las flores

For More Information/Más Información

Books

Grasses. Plants (series). June Loves (Chelsea Clubhouse)

Grasslands. Susan Heinrichs Gray (Compass Point Books)

Libros

Las semillas/Seeds. Heinemann Lee Y Aprende/Heinemann Read and Learn (series). Patricia Whitehouse (Heinemann)

Las raíces/Roots. Heinemann Lee Y Aprende/Heinemann Read and Learn (series). Patricia Whitehouse (Heinemann)

Web Sites/Páginas web

The Great Plant Escape
El Gran Escape de la Planta
www.urbanext.uiuc.edu/gpe
Solve mysteries and learn how plants grow at this fun Web site.
Resuelve misterios y aprende cómo crecen las plantas en esta divertida página web.

Index

Índice

About the Author

Joanne Mattern has written more than 150 books for children. Her favorite things to write about are animals, nature, history, sports, and famous people. Joanne also works in her local library. She lives in New York State with her husband, three daughters, and assorted pets. She enjoys animals, music, going to baseball games, reading, and visiting schools to talk about her books.

Información sobre la autora

Joanne Mattern ha escrito más de 150 libros para niños. Sus temas favoritos son los animales, la naturaleza, la historia, los deportes y la vida de personajes famosos. Además, Joanne trabaja en la biblioteca de su comunidad. Vive en el estado de Nueva York con su esposo, sus tres hijas y varias mascotas. A Joanne le gustan los animales, la música, ir al béisbol, leer y hacer visitas a las escuelas para hablar de sus libros.

24